ETHICAL MACHIAVELLIAN

Mastering the Art of Manipulation for Good

Mohd Faisal

Dedication

To the Almighty God,

Helping us to comprehend and use the complex mechanisms of human influence for the benefit of everyone via His unending wisdom and grace. I pray that this goal will always be noble, right, and consistent with the values of compassion and honesty.

And to You, Dear Reader,

Somebody is responsible for this work's production thanks to their quest for knowledge and dedication to moral perfection. I hope these pages will enlighten you and give you the ability to use the art of manipulation for the benefit of all people. May you always keep in mind the responsibility that comes with having such power—to inspire, to motivate, and to promote positive change—as you make your way through these revelations.

With gratitude and purpose,

~Mohd Faisal

"Men judge generally more by the eye than by the hand, for every-one can see and few can feel. Every one sees what you appear to be, few really know what you are."

- NICCOLÒ MACHIAVELLI

CONTENTS

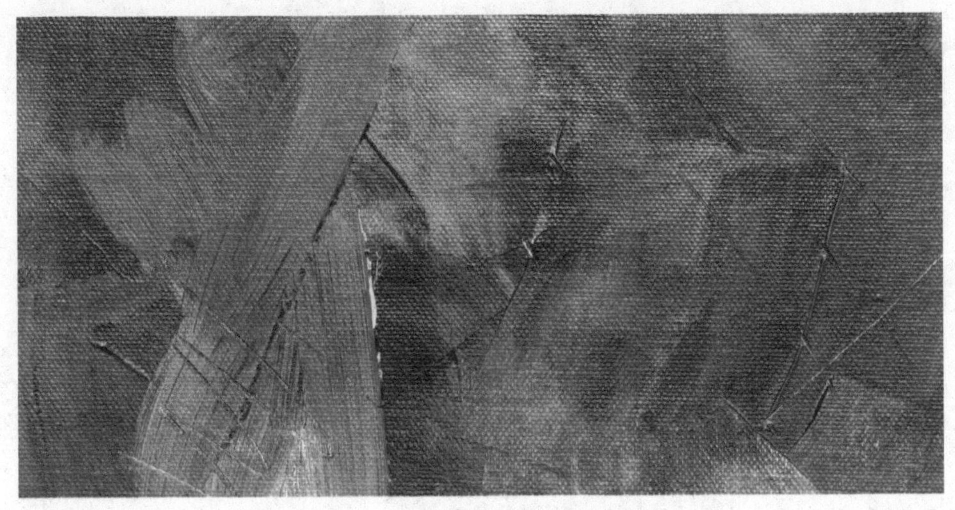

INTRODUCTION

1. Understanding Ethical Manipulation:

Thank you for visiting the fascinating realm of ethical manipulation! Here, we set out on a quest to discover the techniques for using influence skillfully and ethically. In this article, we will investigate the art of persuasive communication while adhering to ethical ideals and principles. You might be wondering, "Can manipulation ever be ethical?" So strap up because we are going to disprove popular wisdom.

Imagine being able to influence individuals to make changes for the better by ethically nudging them in that direction. The goal of ethical manipulation is to use the power of persuasion for good rather than via deception or trickery. Prepare yourself to learn how to use the art of ethical persuasion to change both your personal and professional life.

We'll delve deeply into communication intricacies and the psychology of human behavior on this thrilling voyage. We'll reveal the techniques for creating the three foundations of ethical manipulation: trust, credibility, and empathy. Buckle up because this journey will be filled with exciting revelations, helpful advice, and case studies that will help you become a master of ethical persuasion.

2. The Power Of Ethical Influence:

We reach a critical point in our exploration of ethical manipulation in "The Power of Ethical Influence," where we examine the incredible influence that ethical persuasion can have on both people and societies.

Imagine being able to sincerely motivate people, encouraging them to behave in ways that are consistent with their beliefs and objectives. Your ability to connect with people more deeply is facilitated by ethical influence, which also promotes mutual respect and trust. Utilizing the artistry of storytelling, you may influence people's hearts and minds and bring about significant change for the better.

We will explore the psychology of persuasion strategies and the moral application of emotional appeals. Learn the technique of framing and reframing, where a carefully written message may change viewpoints and lead to positive results. We'll also look at responsible ways to deal with cognitive biases, avoiding manipulation traps and fostering empathy and understanding.

Beyond interpersonal connections, ethical influence has a powerful impact. We'll look at how ethical manipulation may be used in business and leadership settings so that leaders can encourage their employees to have common goals and values. We'll also look into the areas of social impact projects and political debate, where using influence responsibly may be a spark for a better society.

We will stress the significance of upholding integrity and adhering to ethical standards throughout this investigation. The goal of ethical manipulation is empowerment rather than exploitation. By mastering this skill, you may use your influence to promote cooperation, advancement, and harmony.

Prepare yourself to unleash the full power of ethical influence. This chapter will improve your capacity to morally persuade and motivate people. It is jam-packed with interesting thoughts, doable tactics, and insightful case examples. Join us as we leverage ethical manipulation's power for a better and brighter future!

3. Embracing The Machiavellian Mindset:

Ah, the mysterious "Machiavellian Mindset" - a phrase that conjures up ideas of guile, trickery, and intrigue. But do not worry; in order to comprehend ethical manipulation, we must explore the depths of this fascinating thinking and embrace it in a virtuous way.

It's not about engaging in evil plots or immoral tactics to adopt the Machiavellian mindset. It is instead about using Machiavelli's insight to navigate the complexity of human behavior and power relations.

In this chapter, we examine the timeless ideas put forward by the great Italian philosopher Niccol Machiavelli in order to glean important lessons about strategic leadership and decision-making. We'll learn how to use influence while having a thorough grasp of human nature and applying the Machiavellian strategy for the benefit of everyone.

We'll discover how to cultivate a Machiavellian mentality that prioritizes flexibility, pragmatism, and a keen understanding of the subtleties of interpersonal relationships. The Machiavellian style supports a clever assessment of the situation, allowing us to go through trying circumstances with prudence and skill.

But keep in mind that this is not a mandate to act in a Machiavellian manner. Instead, in order to become powerful and influential leaders in both our personal and professional lives, we will choose a principled approach that combines moral principles with Machiavellian insights.

Join us as we unlock the secrets of the Machiavellian Mindset and discover how to use influence and power with morality and integrity. This chapter will provide you the skills you need to adopt the Machiavellian style and use its insight to make a difference in the world. So get ready to accept Machiavelli's ethical spin on his strategic genius!

PREFACE

The search for moral leadership has gained prominence in a time of unparalleled connectedness and complicated power relations. Understanding and influencing human behavior for beneficial results is more important than ever as we navigate a world that is changing quickly. In order to illuminate the complex interactions between manipulation, ethics, and successful leadership, "Ethical Machiavellian: Mastering the Art of Manipulation for Good" was written.

This book's title may generate questions since it combines two ideas that appear incompatible: "Ethical" and "Machiavellian." The Renaissance political philosopher Niccol Machiavelli is frequently linked to cunning and deceit. His writings, especially "The Prince," have been examined and discussed for ages. The focus of this book, however, is on ethical Machiavellianism, a philosophy that uses influence methods for good.

When practiced responsibly, the art of manipulation may be a powerful instrument for accomplishing lofty goals. In this book, we will examine the psychological theories that underlie human decision-making, historical and modern instances of ethical manipulation, and methods for navigating challenging social and professional contexts.

It is crucial to make it clear that the goal of this article is not to encourage manipulation, coercion, or any other negative tactics. Instead, we want to equip individuals with the information they need to navigate complex circumstances, speak clearly, and impact good change. While supporting moral standards and a dedication to the greater good, ethical Machiavellianism promotes knowledge of the dynamics of power and the human mind.

You will come across case studies that show how ethical manipulation has been used to start revolutions, heal cultural gaps, and change people's fates as you read through these chapters. The tales in these pages demonstrate the power of manipulation as a force for good, from political figures who influenced public opinion to social reformers who fought for equality.

This book is an invitation to develop a sophisticated understanding of manipulation—one that recognizes its capacity for constructive change and pushes us to use its strategies responsibly. The trip that lies ahead will need self-awareness, empathy, and a dedication to moral behavior. Let's start a journey to master the art of persuasion for the greater good as we explore the ethical Machiavellianism principles.

May these realizations act as a compass for anyone wishing to influence with compassion, lead with integrity, and foster a society where the deft manipulation of human behavior is used to shape a better future.

The next step is to investigate the ethical Machiavellianism regions, where the practice of virtue and the art of manipulation merge.

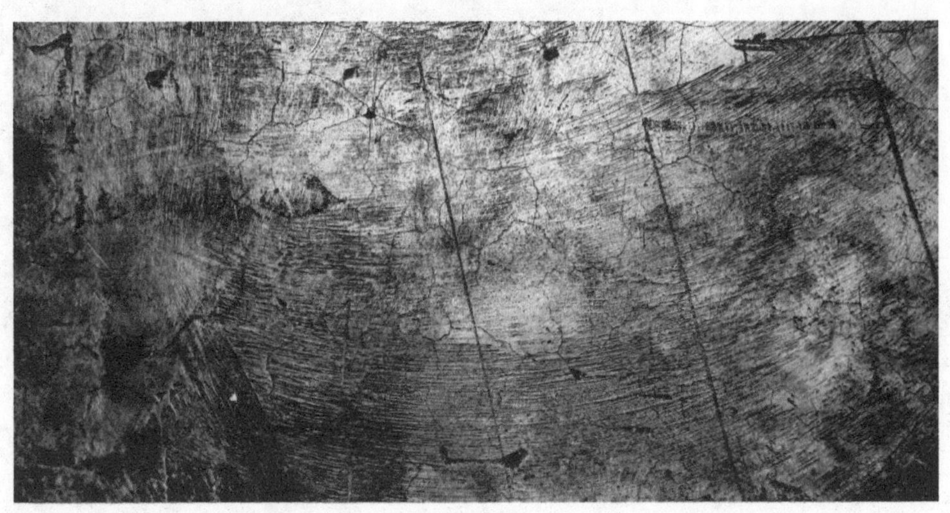

CHAPTER 1: THE FOUNDATION OF ETHICAL MANIPULATION

Identifying Your Values And Ethics:

Good day! So let's discuss defining your morals and ideals. It's like finding the ideal pair of shoes; they should be a great fit for you! But in this instance, it's important to identify the values that speak to you more deeply.

Now imagine that you are at a crossroads with enormous neon signs pointing in all directions. How do you choose which direction to go? One shouts "Integrity," another says "Compassion," and there's one that loudly yells "Honesty."

Now is the moment to reflect on your actions. Consider what is most important to you. Is it showing compassion and respect to others? Is that being sincere even when it's difficult? Or perhaps it's about sticking up for what you stand for, no matter what the circumstances?

Don't misunderstand me; I'm not advocating that you become a philosophical master over night. But being aware of your morals and principles may make all the difference. You may navigate life's maze of options using it as a moral compass.

For a moment, let's be honest. In today's hectic environment, it's simple to overlook what's actually crucial. It's like trying to cling onto slippery soap in the shower. Nevertheless, knowing your values enables you to remain loyal to who you are despite the chaos that may be all around you.

You may be thinking, "Why bother? I'm doing just fine without all this ethical mumbojumbo," but consider yourself a ship traveling through choppy waters without a rudder. Your morals and beliefs serve as your rudder, allowing you to sail over life's choppy waves with style.

The cherry on top is that when you are clear about your principles, making decisions is a piece of cake! Because your guiding principles will point you in the correct route, you won't have to waste time debating what is right or wrong.

Also, being liberated by your ideals is a good thing. It's similar to unleashing your superhero alter ego, such as "Captain Integrity" or "The Honesty Avenger," who is prepared to take on every moral dilemma that arises.

So, my friend, stop for a moment and consider what is most important to you. As you would your closest friend after a long absence, embrace your morals and ideals. They'll be your continuous company and help you stay rooted and loyal to who you are.

Also, let's have some fun with this and give your morals and principles hip names. How about "The Valuesaurus Rex" or "The Code of Awesome"? Personalize it and make it your own!

The adventure to discover your values and ethics is now complete. It's similar like unearthing hidden wealth inside of you. Accept it, value it, and allow it help you become the amazing person you are!

The Role Of Integrity In Ethical Manipulation:

Ah, the fascinating dance between morality and ethical trickery; it's like attempting to walk a tightrope while juggling flames that are on fire! You might be asking yourself, "Wait, isn't manipulation always a bad thing?" Well, no. Let's solve this mystery.

My buddy, integrity is the brilliant shield of your moral integrity. It all comes down to upholding your moral standards despite the temptation to err. Now, when we discuss ethical manipulation, we are not talking about tricking or hurting other people. Instead, it focuses on employing persuasion tactics ethically and openly to produce beneficial results.

Imagine a magician doing a great feat. The magician is aware that the goal is to inspire surprise and amazement, not to take advantage of their audience's trust. The same principles apply to ethical manipulation: it involves persuading people while acting with integrity, empathy, and a sincere desire for their welfare.

Consider that you are a charismatic leader attempting to inspire your group. You use your communication talents to uplift and support others while maintaining respect for their uniqueness and building a sense of trust. That is ethical manipulation in action: utilizing your power to help others while maintaining your moral integrity.

But take care! Manipulation without integrity may go down a dangerous path, much like fire in the wrong hands. It's crucial to evaluate your motivations and make sure they adhere to moral principles. Consider it a yardstick for your behavior: "Does this help others and is it morally right?"

In some cases, ethical manipulation may even entail questioning the status quo in the sake of the larger good. Imagine a strong environmental activist convincing the public and decisionmakers to adopt sustainable practices. That is manipulation motivated by honesty in action, a force for improvement.

So, fellow explorer of ethics and integrity, keep in mind that acting in accordance with your principles gives you actual power. When used with honesty and compassion, ethical manipulation may be a powerful instrument for good.

Let's explore the complexities of ethical manipulation as we go along and the various ways it might be a force for improvement. Let's now explore the art of persuasion and how to morally sway people's opinions in order to improve the world. Take a brave step since the trip has only just begun!

Building Trustworthiness And Credibility:

We now focus on developing trustworthiness and credibility, the foundation of every ethical Machiavellian strategy, in our quest to perfect the art of ethical manipulation for the greater good. Imagine it as building a strong connection with others that is built on the foundations of honesty and integrity.

The most significant asset you have when trying to morally influence someone else is their trust. It resembles a fragile flower that requires care and attention to fully bloom. But how can we foster reliability?

Be a man of your word first and foremost. Deliver on your promises with unrelenting dedication. The cornerstone of trust is reliability, which is developed via consistency. Being trustworthy is necessary if you want others to know they can rely on you.

Another important tool in the arsenal for fostering trust is transparency. It is impossible to exaggerate the value of transparency. You demonstrate to people that you have nothing to hide when you are open and honest about your motives and behavior. It's like to a transparent glass pane that gives people access to your soul.

Let's now discuss credibility, which is a sign of knowledge and experience. You must be seen as a reliable source if you want to morally influence people. Put money into expanding your knowledge and skills. Be knowledgeable, educate yourself, and continue to study and develop. As a beacon, your credibility will radiate and pull others to you.

However, there's still more! In this morallymean Machiavellian quest, empathy is crucial. Recognize the needs, worries, and viewpoints of others. When you approach issues with empathy, other people can tell that you aren't only thinking about yourself and your goals.

Keep in mind that developing credibility and trustworthiness is a process rather than a final goal. It's similar to tending to a blooming garden; ongoing care is necessary to keep it alive and well. The trust you've worked so hard to establish can fall apart with one incorrect action.

As you set out on this journey, remember the strength of integrity, reliability, openness, wisdom, and empathy. Build a solid and enduring bridge of trust with people around you like an expert architect.

We'll discuss the ethical ramifications of persuasive storytelling and the practice of empathic communication in our next chapters. So, continue on this road of mastering manipulation for the greater good while keeping your compass set toward honesty. We move forward!

Establishing Emotional Intelligence And Empathy:

It's time to dig into the critical facets of developing empathy and emotional intelligence as we go forward on our journey to become experts in the art of ethical manipulation for the greater good. These traits give our relationships with others depth and complexity, much like the gentle strokes of an artist.

The capacity to put oneself in another person's shoes for a mile is empathy, my buddy. It's about sharing and comprehending other people's emotions and experiencing the world from their perspective. Empathy training helps us communicate on a fundamental level, overcoming obstacles and building real connections.

While some people are inherently more empathic, it's also a talent that can be developed by deliberate effort. Now, you might be thinking, "Isn't empathy just an inherent trait?" The first phase is active listening, which is genuinely hearing and taking in what people have to say without passing judgment. It's like letting them express themselves freely.

But things don't stop there. Putting oneself in vulnerable situations and being willing to go through emotions with others are further need for empathy. It's like an emotional connection that serves as a reminder that we are all just people navigating the challenges of life together.

Let's now discuss emotional intelligence, which is the ability to recognize, control, and manage our own and others' emotions. Emotional intelligence, like the director of an orchestra, enables us to coordinate our emotions and responses, which improves our ability to communicate and make decisions.

Selfawareness is a crucial component of emotional intelligence. Being aware of our emotions enables us to identify the triggers and biases that might affect our behavior. It's similar to casting a light on our inner landscape, revealing hidden realities and chances for development.

Selfregulation is the skill of keeping calm and preventing emotions from driving impulsive conduct. It's comparable to an experienced sailor guiding the ship through rough waves with calm resolve.

However, emotional intelligence extends beyond selfawareness and selfcontrol. It also includes being aware of and sympathetic to the feelings of others. Like a cultural anthropologist, we pay attention to and decipher the emotional clues of others around us, providing assistance and inspiration as necessary.

As we include empathy and emotional intelligence into our moral Machiavellian strategy, we embrace a deeper comprehension of how people connect with one another. We communicate not just with words but also with empathy and emotional intelligence, like a symphony of understanding.

In the upcoming chapters, we will examine the craft of storytelling and how to use empathy and emotional intelligence to create compelling narratives that motivate people to make changes for the better. Let's thus continue on our journey, embracing the virtues of emotional intelligence and empathy, and developing into moral leaders for a better society. We march forth!

CHAPTER 2: THE ART OF PERSUASION

Understanding Persuasion Techniques:

Ah, the art of persuasion—a balancing act between persuasiveness and morality, like a great conductor guiding an ensemble to a crescendo of uplifting effect. Understanding persuasive strategies develops into a potent weapon in our toolbox as we move forward on our quest to ethical manipulation mastery for the greater good.

My buddy, persuasion is not about forcing or using manipulation to control people. Instead, it's about making strong cases that motivate change while still respecting the autonomy and free choice of individuals we interact with.

Let's speak about the power of storytelling first and foremost. Do you recall the spellbinding stories you read as a youngster that sent your pulse racing and your imagination soar? Storytelling connects with us on an emotional level in a way that facts and data alone can never do.

The idea is that moral narrative must be grounded in reality and honesty. Integrity is key when presenting your ideas. Use stories that speak to your audience's beliefs and objectives. You establish a connection with people that goes beyond the surface level when your stories relate to their own experiences.

The craft of using persuasive words is up next. It's like to a painter expertly picking colors to produce a captivating painting. Respecting the diversity of viewpoints and backgrounds, use your words carefully. Instead of using deceptive words, establish a conversation that values honest, respectful interaction.

Let's now discuss the influence of social proof. Being social animals, humans frequently turn to other people for support and recognition. By highlighting encouraging instances and testimonies that emphasize the advantages of the desired change, ethical persuasion makes use of this phenomena.

Although social proof might be persuasive, it must always be true and correct. So be careful, my fellow traveler. Fabricated endorsements and fraudulent claims damage the ethical basis we've worked so hard to build by eroding confidence.

Let's also investigate the reciprocity principle. Without expecting anything in return, you may foster goodwill and the desire to reciprocate by being nice and helpful. This idea is used by ethical influencers to promote a cooperative environment where everyone gains from constructive interactions.

Not to mention the importance of active listening. It's like a conductor of a symphony, sensitive to every note and ensuring sure no voice is muffled. Pay attention to other people's needs, feedback, and concerns. Show that you genuinely care about their opinions and that you value them.

By embracing the art of persuasion and using ethics as our compass, we improve our capacity to motivate constructive change. The following chapters will examine the difficult balancing act between empathy and assertiveness in communication, bringing us one step closer to being moral influencers who have a longlasting effect. We go on, applying positive persuasion to the ethical manipulation canvas.

Leveraging Reciprocity And Obligation Ethically:

Ah, the fascinating dance of leveraging reciprocity and duty ethically; it's a balance between giving and receiving that always upholds the values of integrity. Understanding these two potent forces is crucial as we move forward in our quest to become experts in ethical manipulation for the greater good.

My buddy, reciprocity is the traditional tenet of "give and you shall receive." Our ethical philosophy, however, does not involve giving with the hope of receiving anything in return. Instead, it's about actually providing compassion and value in order to start a chain reaction of trust and goodwill.

Imagine lending someone a helping hand with no conditions attached. It's comparable to sowing a generous seed that blossoms into a lovely tree of uplifting impact. The power of reciprocity comes into play because people are more prone to interact with individuals who have been good to them.

Leveraging reciprocity should never be used as a kind of manipulation, therefore let's proceed cautiously. Building genuine relationships and developing a feeling of community are key. Giving freely and selflessly fosters a culture of mutual support where everyone gains from the goodwill of the group.

Let's now investigate the area of ethical duty. Although it may appear to be a great weight, it is more about the obligation we feel to people we have the power to affect. The ethical duty we have to uphold serves as a reminder to put other people's needs first and behave in their best interests.

We must be conscious of how our activities could affect other people in our capacity as moral influences. Balancing our ambitions with the effects on those we touch is like walking a tightrope. Our decisions are shaped by this knowledge, ensuring that they follow our moral compass.

Recall that openness is essential for effectively utilizing duty and reciprocity. Always be honest about your motives and avoid using these rules to control or take advantage of people. Understanding your intentions helps build trust and bolsters the moral base of your influence.

In addition, applying empathy is crucial when following these guidelines. Consider the needs and ambitions of individuals you engage with, and put yourself in their position. This empathic approach equips you to use duty and reciprocity for the common good rather than selfish ends.

Let's keep the inner fires of responsibility and reciprocity blazing as we proceed along our moral Machiavellian path. We exemplify the genuine meaning of ethical influence by giving unselfishly, encouraging trust, and understanding our responsibilities to others.

The complexities of ethical negotiating and the skill of striking a balance between aggressiveness and sensitivity will be covered in our upcoming chapters. So, bearing the light of responsibility and reciprocity, we advance, illuminating the way of ethical manipulation for the greater good.

The Art Of Framing And Reframing:

Ah, the art of framing and reframing; it's like a great painter picking the ideal angle to produce a mesmerizing masterpiece. Understanding these strategies becomes a potent weapon in our ethical arsenal as we advance in our quest to master the art of ethical manipulation for the greater good.

It's all about presenting information in a way that affects how others see it, my buddy, and that's what framing is all about. It's like preparing the stage for a potent performance when the focus is on the elements we want to highlight.

In order to frame anything ethically, you must do so in a responsible, open manner without trying to manipulate others. It involves accurately presenting information and concepts while purposefully emphasizing the beneficial effects they may have on people or society.

Consider that you are trying to raise support for a worthwhile cause. By highlighting the potential advantages your cause might have for the neighborhood, ethical framing encourages others to join the group effort for positive change.

But keep in mind that moral influencers never deceive by embellishing the truth or offering a biased viewpoint. Respecting our audience's individuality and intellect requires us to structure information in an honest and genuine way.

Let's now examine the power of reframing, a strategy that may alter perspectives and create new opportunities. It's similar to taking a fresh look at a familiar area to see its hidden beauty and promise.

We help people view things differently by rephrasing circumstances responsibly. It could entail forging a sense of oneness, bringing opposing groups together, or stressing ideals that encourage collaboration.

As moral influencers, we employ reframing to handle delicate subjects with care and empathy. It involves turning obstacles into chances and disagreements into constructive talks.

Let's be careful, though; reframing shouldn't be used to control or deceive. It involves delivering authentic, truthful, and alternate viewpoints that provide a deeper comprehension of difficult problems.

As we master the craft of ethical framing and reframing, we advance as storytellers and designers of tales that spur constructive change. We establish a connection with our audience's ideals and objectives by talking openly and empathetically.

The ethics of influence and persuasion under delicate circumstances will be covered in more detail in the next chapters. Let's therefore embrace the art of framing and reframing with integrity since it has the potential to change people's thoughts and the planet. We continue, laying down broad strokes of framing and reframing for the sake of the larger good on the canvas of ethical manipulation.

Navigating Cognitive Biases For Positive Outcomes:

Ah, the intriguing realm of cognitive biases—those psychological oddities that have the power to both lead and mislead us on our morally ambiguous Machiavellian quest. Understanding and overcoming these biases become crucial in obtaining successful results as we work to perfect the art of ethical manipulation for the greater good.

Cognitive biases, my friend, are akin to little information processing short cuts that our brains make. While they might aid us in making rapid judgments, if not used correctly, they can also cause us to make the wrong choices.

Confirmation bias is a prevalent prejudice that refers to the propensity to favor data that supports our prior ideas. Influencers who uphold ethics must be on the lookout for this prejudice. Instead, we encourage an openminded approach to decisionmaking by seeking out many viewpoints and challenging our own presumptions.

The halo effect is another fascinating bias, where our general opinion of a person affects how we perceive their unique traits. Being aware that someone's charisma or appeal does not always imply their trustworthiness or ethical standing, ethical influencers maintain their vigilance.

We also meet the availability heuristic, whereby we base our conclusions on instances that are easily accessible. We must refrain from using this prejudice to advance a certain goal in order to prevent ethical manipulation. Instead, we give a balanced viewpoint and provide background information to properly enlighten our readers.

Let's now discuss the anchoring bias, which is the propensity to place a lot of weight on the initial piece of information that is encountered. The use of excessive or prejudiced starting points must be avoided by ethical influencers. Instead, we aim to offer a balanced and wideranging set of facts to support wise decisionmaking.

The selfserving bias, when we ascribe favorable results to our skills and poor ones to external forces, is another prejudice that is worthwhile studying. Honest influencers must own up to their errors and accept responsibility for their behavior.

We empower ourselves with information and selfawareness as we negotiate the difficult terrain of cognitive biases. We must be aware of our own and other people's prejudices in order to avoid using them against them or manipulating them for our own

benefit.

Additionally, empathy is essential in this situation. Understanding how cognitive biases affect people's perceptions and choices allows us to craft our messages with compassion and sensitivity, guiding recipients toward morally sound outcomes.

We'll examine how ethics and decisionmaking interact in the upcoming chapters, learning how to avoid cognitive biases while acting morally and honorably. So let's embrace the craft of ethical manipulation, be aware of the mental biases that mold us, and give ourselves the capacity to bring about constructive change in the world. We move forward, navigating the complexities of cognitive biases to permanently perfect the technique.

CHAPTER 3:
THE POWER OF STORYTELLING

Crafting Compelling And Ethical Narratives:

Ah, the alluring realm of creating morally and ethically sound stories that attract readers while respecting the values of authenticity and integrity. It's like building a tapestry of words. Understanding how to craft stories that spur positive change becomes an essential ability as we go on our path to mastering the art of ethical manipulation for the greater good.

My buddy, an engaging tale is a potent instrument that has a significant impact on our audience. They are drawn into the tale as if by a magical spell, becoming active players in the adventure we want to take together.

But how can we create such stories in an ethical manner? Truth serves as the first and main building block of all engaging stories, so let's start there. Facts are never twisted or made up by ethical influencers. Instead, we believe in the power of true stories, examples from everyday life, and trustworthy information.

Another important component is transparency. Think of the truth as the crystalclear lake that our story is reflecting. The audience may confidently and clearly navigate the seas of our tale thanks to the context that ethical storytellers supply and the disclosure of any potential biases.

Additionally, the construction of ethical tales heavily relies on empathy. We put ourselves in our audience's position to better comprehend their objectives, concerns, and dreams. We are guided by this empathic perspective as we craft storylines that speak to their emotions and resonate with their beliefs.

Let's now discuss the craft of storytelling as a whole. The use of narrative to motivate change for the greater good is embraced by ethical influencers. Our stories develop into vehicles that convey important ideas, inspiring action and building a sense of solidarity in our common goal.

But let's not forget that our stories are not instruments of control or compulsion. By empowering people to make knowledgeable decisions, ethical storytelling respects their individuality and free will. Instead of pulling people along against their will, it's about welcoming them on a trip.

We increase our power to effect change when we create engaging and moral narratives. Our narratives serve as change agents, creating a desire in our audience to make the world a better place.

Using tales for Connection and Influence: Ah, the alluring power of tales. They're like bridges that link people's hearts and brains, giving us the power to morally influence and motivate good deeds. Harnessing the beauty of narrative becomes a powerful weapon in our journey as we explore deeper into the practice of ethical manipulation for the greater good.

Stories, my friend, are the secret to building trust with our audience. It seems like a loving hug that welcomes them into a world of common feelings and experiences.

Storytelling has the power to alter, according to ethical influencers. Instead of using them to deceive or manipulate, we utilize them to promote real empathy and understanding. By serving as vehicles for inspiration and truth, our stories encourage others to join us on the road to progress.

The capacity of storytelling to cut beyond linguistic, cultural, and religious barriers is one of its most powerful qualities. A well constructed tale reaches into the spirit, creating a connection that binds us all as fellow passengers on this trip called life.

But how can we responsibly utilize tales to affect favorable outcomes? Our main priority is to embrace genuineness. Our stories are based on the truth and use relevant circumstances and reallife experiences. Achieving an advantage never requires ethical influencers to lie or exaggerate.

Our compass continues to be empathy. We put ourselves in our audience's shoes to better comprehend their delights, challenges, and objectives. We can create tales that appeal to their emotions and motivate people to act for the greater good thanks to this sympathetic connection.

By never forcing our opinions or values on our audience, ethical storytelling also empowers them. Instead, we encourage kids to come to their own conclusions by basing their choices on the tales we tell.

We develop as storytellers of truth and empathy as we utilize tales for connection and impact. Our stories serve as change agents and lighthouses of hope, blazing the way to a happier, more kind world.

Ethical Use Of Emotional Appeals:

Ah, the delicate art of ethically harnessing the force of emotional appeals—it's like taming a wild stallion, using its might for good without doing damage. Knowing how to use emotional appeals ethically becomes increasingly important in our journey as we develop our grasp of ethical manipulation for the greater good.

My friend, emotional appeals touch our audience's heartstrings. They are a symphony of feelings that can arouse empathy, compassion, and the desire to take constructive action. Ethical influencers understand that while emotions may be a strong force for change, they must be used carefully and with integrity.

Authenticity is the primary tenet of ethical emotional appeals. We must demonstrate sincere feelings derived from actual encounters and sincere goals. Emotional manipulation for selfish reasons or to deceive others is a clear violation of moral standards.

Furthermore, ethical influencers do not manipulate others' weaknesses or emotional triggers to change their minds. Our goal is to interact respectfully and compassionately with our audience while fostering bonds built on mutual respect and understanding.

Transparency serves as our beacon of hope. When using emotional appeals, we are transparent about our goals and the feelings we hope to arouse. Our target audience deserves to understand the intentions behind our messaging so that they may make wise judgments.

We also acknowledge the variety of feelings and reactions our audience may exhibit. Ethical emotional appeals encourage our audience to think and feel for themselves rather than attempting to impose a single emotional stance.

The foundation of ethical influence is still empathy. We must be sensitive to and compassionate toward our audience by being aware of their emotional terrain. Ethical influencers utilize emotional appeals to build bonds of understanding rather than to control or alienate.

We become stewards of emotions as we employ emotional appeals in an ethical manner, directing them toward motivating constructive change. Inspiring action toward a more compassionate and just society, our messages serve as stimuli for empathy and compassion.

Engaging The Power Of Symbols And Metaphors:

Ah, the appeal of symbols and metaphors, like secret codes that open the door to our audience's knowledge and imagination. Utilizing the influence of symbols and metaphors develops into a powerful weapon in our toolbox as we continue on our journey to being ethical manipulation masters for the greater good.

Symbols, my friend, have deep significance that goes beyond language. They evoke feelings and experiences that are profoundly engraved in our minds, like mystical runes inscribed in the fabric of our collective consciousness.

Ethical influencers are aware of the power of metaphors and symbols. We utilize them to communicate complicated concepts and beliefs in a way that genuinely connects with our audience, not to manipulate or deceive. Our use of symbols is openended, encouraging the audience to give them their own distinctive interpretations.

On the other hand, metaphors provide a bridge between dissimilar ideas, making the abstract real and approachable. They act as vivid mental pictures painted by poetic strokes, enhancing the impact and recall of our words.

But how can we use metaphors and symbols in an ethical way? We make sure they are first and foremost clear to everyone and sensitive to cultural differences. Symbols that can unintentionally insult or alienate particular communities are avoided by ethical influencers. We want to employ symbols that promote inclusion and togetherness instead.

Additionally, we refrain from using deceptive strategies like inciting fear or stirring up strong emotions for our own benefit. Our aim is to elevate and inspire, utilizing images and metaphors to foster a common vision of progress.

We still see transparency as being our guiding philosophy. We are transparent about the meaning of the symbols and metaphors we use and how they connect to our ethical message. We ask the audience to join us on the symbolic trip and make their own connections.

There is also a big part for empathy in this. Utilizing symbols and metaphors that are relatable to our audience's experiences and ideals requires an understanding of their cultural and emotional context.

By responsibly utilizing the power of symbols and metaphors, we develop into mental storytellers who can create narratives that go beyond the bounds of words. Our messages acquire a deeper significance as a result, encouraging the audience to picture a united and hopeful future.

We'll go more into the ethics of persuasion and the practice of courteous communication in the upcoming chapters. So let's continue to embrace the power of symbols and metaphors and use them to open the doors to empathy and understanding as we travel the path of ethical manipulation for the greater good. We go forward under the effect of symbolism and the artistic ethical influence.

CHAPTER 4: INFLUENCING THROUGH COMMUNICATION

Effective Communication Strategies:

Ah, the techniques for ethical manipulation through good communication are like using a wellbalanced, expertly built sword. Learning strong communication skills becomes increasingly important as we progress in our quest to master ethical manipulation for the common good.

The basis of moral influence, my friend, is effective communication. Our audience is captivated by it, and it moves them to support us in bringing about great change. It's like a dance of words and body language.

The word "exploit" may have negative connotations, but in the context of ethical manipulation, it refers to using opportunities ethically and honestly, always keeping the interests of the larger good in mind.

Active listening is, first and foremost, a superpower in communication. We must pay attention to the wants, desires, and goals of our audience while displaying real interest and empathy. We build a sense of connection and trust—the cornerstones of ethical influence—by genuinely listening to them.

Transparency continues to be our compass. Influencers that uphold ethics are transparent about their goals, intentions, and desired effects. Secrets have no place in ethical manipulation since we openly discuss our objectives and methods with our audience, enabling them to make educated decisions.

Our communication techniques continue to be guided by empathy. We can better customize our messages with compassion and empathy if we are aware of the emotions and viewpoints of our audience. Our words build bridges of communication rather than barriers of separation.

A crucial function is played by language. Aware of the variety of viewpoints, ethical influencers use their words carefully and steer clear of deceptive terminology. We strive for simplicity and eliminate ambiguity to make sure that everyone can access and comprehend our communications.

Additionally, we use narrative as a potent technique for communication. Moral stories grab readers' hearts and minds, making difficult concepts approachable and motivating them to take action. We develop a common vision through tales that binds us together in the quest of constructive change.

We become into persuasive defenders of the greater good when we develop effective communication techniques for ethical manipulation. Our words serve as a source of inspiration, pointing people in the direction of a future characterized by honesty, understanding, and compassion.

Building Rapport And Connection Ethically:

Establishing Trust and Connection In terms of ethics, developing rapport and connections with others ethically is a key step on our path to mastering ethical manipulation for the greater good. Let's investigate ways to establish real connections without using covert or manipulative methods as we work to inspire good change.

Active listening is, first and foremost, a potent instrument for ethical rapportbuilding. We foster an environment of trust and openness when we pay close attention to people and sincerely try to comprehend their viewpoints. Consider the situation of working on a group project for the community. Give each team member your undivided attention as you hear out their thoughts and issues, showing them that you value and appreciate their contributions.

The basis of ethical connectedness is empathy. We develop empathy and understanding by placing ourselves in other people's situations and comprehending their feelings and experiences. Think of a scenario where you are working with a group of people from various backgrounds. Encourage a feeling of tolerance and togetherness by recognising and embracing their distinctive cultural viewpoints.

Honesty and transparency are driving ideals. Avoid having any secret motives and be open and honest about your objectives. For instance, if you're promoting a cause or project, be open about the initiative's ultimate objective and how it fits with the advancement of the neighborhood or society at large.

Respecting diversity is crucial to developing moral relationships. Recognize each person's individuality and treat them with respect. Respect diverse viewpoints in the workplace and create an atmosphere where healthy disagreements may result in creative solutions.

Authenticity is a potent link. Be sincere in your dealings and be loyal to who you are and your ideals. People who are consistent in their words and behavior are more likely to inspire trust and a sense of connection.

Finding points of agreement might help to enhance the rapport. Identify common interests or objectives and use them as a foundation for cooperation and comprehension. Seek for winwin solutions, for instance, in commercial negotiations that take into account the interests of all parties.

The use of nonverbal clues and body language also aid in ethical bonding. Keep your body language open and upbeat so that it comes out as friendly and approachable. To avoid seeming manipulative or untruthful, avoid replicating body language for no other reason than to establish rapport.

In conclusion, developing true understanding, empathy, and respect is key to developing rapport and connection in an ethical manner. Our relationships become genuine and meaningful when we approach people in this way. This propels us toward having an ethical impact that leads to constructive change.

We'll examine the nuances of moral bargaining and the value of empathic communication in the upcoming chapters. Let's continue on this path, building relationships based on trust and compassion that support our goal of moral manipulation for the benefit of everyone. We advance while being directed by the values of moral rectitude and genuine connection.

The Art Of Active Listening:

The skill of active listening shines as a priceless jewel in our influence's crown in the magical world of ethical manipulation for the greater good. Adopting this talent enables us to communicate with people on a deeper level, promoting an atmosphere of trust and understanding.

Active listening, my friend, is a collaborative and compassionate dance of understanding rather than only hearing words. We show that other people's opinions and feelings are important to us by listening carefully to what they have to say.

Imagine yourself participating in a collaborative effort to address social concerns in your neighborhood. Giving each team member enough room to express their ideas without interruptions or judgements would be an ethical influencer's role in active listening. You may appreciate someone by proactively appreciating their contributions.

Additionally, thoughtful listening is a potent weapon in our ethical toolbox. It serves as a mirror, validating the speaker's feelings and thoughts as they are spoken. For instance, you may use reflective listening to react when someone raises worries about environmental sustainability by stating, "I understand that you feel passionately about preserving our environment and creating a greener future."

By utilizing this compelling technique of active listening, we establish a secure and encouraging environment for candid communication. It encourages people to express their thoughts and worries, establishing a collaborative and imaginative environment.

Active listening also aids in identifying underlying motives and requirements. For instance, while talking to project stakeholders, their verbal and nonverbal clues may indicate that they want to have a social effect or advance personally. By paying close attention as they speak, we may adjust our strategy to suit their goals.

As we develop ethical active listening skills, we improve our capacity for sincere human connection. It gives us the chance to develop deep connections and hone our plans for bringing about change.

We'll explore the power of narrative and the ethics of influence in the next chapters. We go on a journey toward deeper empathy and understanding by including active listening into our toolset for ethical manipulation. We advance, led by the soothing melody of attentive listening and sympathetic persuading.

Ethical Use Of Body Language And Nonverbal Cues:

Ah, the delicious dance of body language and nonverbal clues those clandestine messages we send out like undercover spies on a mission. Let's investigate how to use these cues in a way that leaves our audience both enthralled and knowledgeable as we explore the world of ethical manipulation for the greater good.

Imagine that you are engaged in a crucial discussion with the goal of gaining support for a socially beneficial initiative. Your body language becomes your dependable partner as an ethical influencer, conveying assurance and sincerity without using words. The ideal superhero combination that immediately puts other people at ease is a solid handshake and a genuine grin.

Here's a funny but real fact: body language is louder than words, like a rock band playing at maximum volume. Moral influencers are aware that their nonverbal clues can either be a brilliant display of reliability or a disorganized eruption of distrust.

Let's thus have a fun journey into the world of nonverbal communication. It's like serving someone the most delicious slice of cake at the party when you lean forward and show a sincere interest in what they have to say. People are captivated to your alert demeanor and inwardly think, "Wow, this person really cares!"

However, there's still more! Crossing your arms and twitching like a caffeinefueled squirrel is like giving others permission to think you're withdrawn or worried. Like a clumsy dancer avoids falling over their own feet, an ethical influencer stays away from these accidental negative messages.

We have a handy little tool in our ethical toolkit called mirroring. It's like a ninja technique when you can mimic someone else's body language and facial emotions to instantly establish a connection. Be careful, though; mirroring must be subtle and genuine rather than a creepy impersonation that raises red flags with your audience.

The ability to maintain eye contact while holding a strong hand of poker is yet another treasure. Eye contact is a sign of respect and participation among ethical influencers, but not in a way that makes others feel questioned.

Remember that our actions speak louder than words as we explore the world of moral body language and nonverbal clues. We weave these nonverbal enchantments like a master magician to establish rapport, trust, and connection with our audience.

We'll discuss the ethics of persuasion and the craft of narrative in the future chapters. So, let's give our body language and nonverbal clues some flare, my fellow ethical manipulators, to make them a potent ally in our pursuit of good change. We march forward, flaunting our moral superiority like peacocks and leaving a trail of alluring clues in our wake.

CHAPTER 5: ETHICAL MACHIAVELLIAN LEADERSHIP

Ethical Leadership Traits And Styles:

Ladies and gentlemen, when we discuss ethical leadership qualities and styles, we start down a path that is really important. Embodying characteristics that motivate people to achieve greatness is what ethical leadership is all about; it is more than just having a title or being in charge.

Imagine a leader who exudes honesty, like a beacon illuminating a path across stormy waters. The trust of their team and followers is earned by ethical leaders by upholding honesty and openness, which acts as a soother for tired hearts.

Friends, let me tell you something: ethical leadership is not a onesizefitsall proposition. Each of the many styles is weaved with its own special qualities. Some leaders take a humble approach to leading, listening to their team members' opinions like a sage and learning from the group's collective experience.

Others exhibit courage, taking on obstacles headon like a brave warrior and bravely defending their team. Their courage serves as a shining example for others, inspiring them to overcome hardship.

Empathy is a key component of ethical leadership, as does acting as a kind of caring mentor to people we are in charge of. These leaders promote an atmosphere of empathy and support by being aware of the concerns and hopes of their team.

Imagine a leader who welcomes variety and inclusion like a painter would a colorful canvas. Aware that unity results from the symphony of various voices, ethical leaders appreciate the diversity of viewpoints.

However, there's still more! A dynamic factor in the ethical environment is adaptive leadership. Adaptive leaders steer their teams through choppy waters with elegance and endurance, adjusting their sails to the shifting winds like a skillful navigator.

Friends, let's not forget about transformative leadership. These managers inspire their teams to strive for the stars by projecting their ambitions over the horizon like visionaries. Their fans are inspired by their enthusiasm, which motivates them to do remarkable things.

Therefore, the constant dedication to helping others that unites every ethical leader is the common thread that runs through them all, regardless of whether they are leading with humility, bravery, empathy, inclusion, flexibility, or change.

We'll examine the nuances of ethical influence and the craft of persuasive communication in the upcoming chapters. Therefore, let us embrace these admirable qualities and leadership styles as the guiding light that shows the way to a better future, my fellow passengers on this voyage of ethical leadership. Moving forward, we leave a lasting impression on people we lead, like a wellbalanced orchestra performing the symphony of ethical leadership.

Empowering Others Through Influence:

Using our influence to inspire others is similar to sowing the seeds of greatness in the minds of people who are close to us. Let's investigate the art of uplifting people and igniting their potential as we go on our quest to being ethical manipulation masters for the greater good.

Imagine an ethical leader who, like a competent gardener uncovering hidden blooms on a tree, recognizes the unrealized potential and desires of their team. They have faith in other people's skills, which fosters growth and creates an environment that is favorable to achievement.

The beauty of influence, though, is that it involves supporting and leading people rather than commanding or directing them. A genuine sense of empowerment comes from letting people succeed on their own terms, ethical influencers are aware of this.

Imagine a leader who, like a kind mentor, generously imparts wisdom to their followers by sharing their knowledge and skills. Sharing does not lessen their strength; rather, it increases it as they build a network of strong individuals.

Friends, let's now discuss the impact of encouragement. The same way a bright sun fills a garden with light, ethical influencers pull others up with words of encouragement and acknowledgment. Their comments foster a positive and expanding culture by instilling a sense of confidence and belonging.

Effective communication also turns into a potent instrument for empowering others. A caring confidant, ethical influencers carefully listen in order to comprehend the needs and goals of their team. They may adapt their messaging to motivate action and advancement by developing a strong connection.

However, there's still more! Like a kind benefactor presenting priceless diamonds, ethical influences open doors for advancement. They are aware that supporting the development of others is a contribution to the larger good.

Through our influence, we may enable others to make great

changes, which has a farreaching positive impact. It's similar like burning candles in the dark to make a route visible for others to follow.

Fostering A Culture Of Ethics And Integrity:

Promoting a culture of ethics and integrity is similar to caring for the roots of a strong tree because it grounds our activities in timeless morals. Fostering an ethical culture becomes a crucial pillar of our journey as we negotiate the ethical manipulation landscape for the greater good.

Imagine a company whose moral principles serve as the cornerstone, much like a strong foundation does to sustain a grand castle. Honesty, openness, and responsibility are valued highly in this culture and serve as the benchmarks for all choices and actions.

The beauty of encouraging an ethical and moral culture is that it involves more than simply establishing regulations; it also involves motivating people. Leaders who uphold moral standards are aware that their values infiltrate an organization's fundamental core when they are lived and breathed.

Imagine a place of work where everyone is respected and treated with dignity, much like a garden thriving with a variety of vivid flowers. A culture of inclusion is created by ethical influencers who foster a climate in which diversity is appreciated and everyone's opinion is heard.

Friends, let's now discuss the effectiveness of setting a good example. Influencers who uphold ethics do more than just speak the talk; they also act with integrity, paving the way for others to follow. Their actions serve as a compass, pointing the route to moral behavior.

A culture of ethics also promotes free communication, which is like a river of ideas and criticism flowing. A culture where concerns may be expressed without fear of retaliation is fostered by ethical influencers who open up avenues for open dialogue.

However, there's still more! Ethical influencers take a position against unethical activity, acting as a valiant defender of the culture's sacredness. They sustain moral standards even when presented with morally challenging choices, not only when it's easy to do so.

We create an atmosphere where people are empowered to make moral decisions on their own as we nurture an ethical and moral culture. It's similar to taking care of a forest where each tree stands tall and adds to the beauty and power of the whole.

Balancing Ethical Manipulation With Authenticity:

Oh, my dear seeker of knowledge, you walk a fine line as you attempt to master the art of ethical manipulation without sacrificing authenticity. Such a trip calls for a reasonable strategy, one that respects the admirable goals that reside in your heart. Pay close attention since I'll be sharing some wise advice with you.

Remember that your motives must always be in line with the greater good in this world of ethical influence since manipulations devoid of virtue often end in failure. Try to inspire and encourage people rather than using them for your own selfish benefit. Your goal should be to act as a kind guide who gently leads others along the road of development and enlightenment.

Your single word and deed must be built on authenticity, which is like a gleaming pearl. Wearing a mask of deceit or wearing false facades will only cause them to fall apart eventually, exposing the hollowness behind. Instead, accept who you really are—flawed but genuine—because it is only through sincerity that longlasting relationships can grow and trust can be built.

Never lose sight of the responsibility that is on your shoulders when you use the art of manipulation for good. Be aware of the implications of your activities and consider how they could affect other people's life in a cascade. Instead of attempting to impose your will by force, try to convince others through logic and empathy while letting them come to their own conclusions.

As the ancient sages used to say, "The road to virtue is not a straight path, but one with many winding turns." Be ready for obstacles and temptations that will put your dedication to moral methods to the test while you pursue your goal. Let your moral compass lead you through the darkest of nights by being steadfast.

Never forget that genuine mastery comes from managing oneself rather than other people, dear seeker. Accept humility because it helps you avoid being arrogant and paves the way for real interactions with the people you want to influence.

May the light of authenticity guide your search for ethical manipulation, and may you emerge as a positive influencer who has grace and wisdom to impact the lives of many. May the grandeur of virtue and the warmth of honesty accompany you on your travels.

CHAPTER 6: ETHICAL INFLUENCE IN ACTION

Applying Ethical Manipulation In Personal Relationships:

Oh, my dear reader, the subtleties of using ethical manipulation in interpersonal interactions are like the subtle and profound dance of light upon the ocean. As you set out on this noble road, keep in mind that the art of influence must be used with the utmost care and compassion since the seeds of ethical manipulation can be sowed only within the confines of trust and honesty.

Take care of the empathy and understanding soil in the garden of relationships. Try to understand the thoughts and feelings of others nearby while enjoying each person's own personality. Your intentions can only be driven by the desire to inspire and empower others when you genuinely connect with them on a heartfelt level.

Dear reader, the foundation of this trip is patience. Avoid acting hastily while using your influence since doing so might result in unforeseen effects. Instead, spend time learning about the currents that run through each person's heart and let your impact be like the calm wind that gently sways a tree's leaves.

Honesty and transparency must be the guiding lights that show you the way. Do not let the gloom of lying obscure your intentions since trust is the tenuous cord that connects people's hearts. When you speak honestly, your words will carry the weight of authenticity, creating understanding and establishing ties that survive the test of time.

Be a source of inspiration and support in all your encounters. Encourage others to reach their own greatness by fanning their own inspiration's flames. Always keep in mind that helping people identify their own skills and abilities is more important than forcing them to conform to your will.

However, be careful not to fall victim to the tempting attraction of manipulation for personal benefit as you negotiate the landscape of ethical manipulation. Stay faithful to the principles that are at the center of who you are, and allow your moral compass serve as your compass for direction. This will help to ensure that your impact is firmly rooted in the pursuit of the greater good.

You could occasionally trip and fall on this path since human error is common. When you do, embrace humility, admitting your errors and making apologies while really repentant.

According to ancient sages, "To wield the power of influence ethically is to dance in harmony with the universe." May you lead the way for positive change and create a symphony of kindness and compassion in the lives of everyone you come in contact with.

Let grace, wisdom, and the brilliance of integrity guide you as you work to perfect the art of ethical manipulation in interpersonal interactions, dear reader.

Ethical Influence In Business And Negotiations:

Ah, my reader, the pursuit of ethical influence bears significant relevance in the context of business and negotiations. Let's keep the knowledge of the past in mind as we negotiate the complex pathways of business and engagement, and let's aim for moral behavior.

It is crucial to consider how our actions could affect other people in these interactions. Build relationships based on respect and trust rather than manipulating or lying. Sustainable collaborations that last the test of time will be enabled by open and honest communication.

Dear reader, beware of the seduction of shady methods and quick cuts. Even while they can appear to offer quick advantages, they frequently result in longterm regret and a damaged image. Accepting the route of integrity can help you find your way through even the most difficult situations.

Keep in mind that negotiations are chances to seek mutual gain and peace rather than fights to be won at any costs. Look for areas of agreement, comprehension, and sympathetic care for the interests of all parties.

Develop empathy and compassion if you want to influence people in an ethical way. Recognize and respect other people's viewpoints and interests. By doing this, you may develop solutions that meet everyone's needs, encouraging cooperation and a sense of success.

Dear reader, embrace your inner strength, but utilize it wisely and righteously. Instead of controlling people, give them the tools they need to succeed. You will find your own rise to greater heights through elevating others.

The ability to manipulate is not the ultimate test of a great master of this craft, dear reader; rather, it is the ability to motivate constructive change. If you choose the right course, your influence will extend well beyond any bargaining table.

Ethical Use of Manipulation in Social Impact Initiatives:

Ah, my reader, the idea of ethical manipulation may appear counterintuitive when it comes to social impact efforts. Let's instead explore the fundamental knowledge that underlies this idea.

One must be cautious and alert when pursuing great goals. If there is such a thing as ethical manipulation, it should be used to achieve beneficial results for the greater benefit. This calls for a strong sense of accountability and a sincere dedication to the well-being of the people we want to serve.

Let us keep in mind that manipulation is not necessarily bad as we begin these activities. Its moral standing is determined by the motivation behind its usage. As a result, dear reader, our motivations must be driven by empathy, compassion, and a sincere desire to improve both society as a whole and individual lives.

Any social impact program should continue to be guided by the notion of transparency. We must be open and honest about our goals, processes, and anticipated results. Gaining the confidence of our stakeholders guarantees that our decisions are made with honesty and that our actions are consistent with our stated objectives.

The ethical use of manipulation also means giving individuals we want to assist more power, dear reader. We should promote their agency and autonomy rather than forcing our will on them. Since the impacted communities take on a more active role in shaping their own development, this empowerment may result in lon-glasting transformation.

We must guard against the desire to manipulate for our own benefit or to promote secret objectives as we walk this fine line, though. Individual interests should never take precedence over the welfare of others. Keep in mind that improving society is the ultimate goal of all of our efforts.

Let us embrace humility and lifelong learning as we work to perfect the art of ethical manipulation for good, dear reader. Keep an open mind to other viewpoints since it is only through cooperation and group knowledge that we can actually bring about dramatic change.

In conclusion, remember that ethical manipulation may have a beneficial effect when used with good intentions, despite the fact that it may seem counterintuitive. Let us use this power carefully as we work to make the world a better and more just place for everyone, always conscious of the moral ramifications of our choices.

Ethical Manipulation In Politics And Public Discourse:

Dear Reader, the idea of ethical manipulation in political and public conversation is one that is difficult and complex. Even while the word "manipulation" frequently conjures up negative images, there are times when it may be used morally to advance the interests of society and encourage constructive change.

Political manipulation that adheres to the ethics of truthfulness, openness, and respect for democratic norms involves the art of persuasion and influence. Instead than seeking to confuse or mislead the audience, it focuses on enabling people to make educated decisions.

The ethical use of speech and message is a key component of political manipulation. Leaders and public personalities must be careful with their words and arguments, making sure they are based in reality and not motivated by malice or selfish interests. Honest communication builds trust, and trust is the cornerstone of a successful democracy.

Additionally, ethical manipulation entails appealing to societal norms and ambitions that are held in common. Instead of fostering division or sowing dissension, leaders who want to see good change can encourage optimism, unity, and a feeling of purpose among their followers.

Maintaining moral standards in politics and public debate requires transparency. Gaining the public's trust requires leaders to be transparent about their intentions, objectives, and decision-making procedures. Disillusionment and societal division can result from hidden goals and covert tactics, which undermine democracy at its core.

A strong dedication to critical thinking and abstaining from manipulation for one's own advantage or immediate success are also necessary for ethical manipulation. Instead, it emphasizes long-term viable solutions that take into account the actual demands and concerns of the populace.

As citizens, it is our duty to hold our elected officials responsible for their words and deeds. To protect the credibility of our political institutions and public debate, we must be vigilant against deceptive strategies that undercut the democratic process.

Ultimately, dear reader, ethical manipulation in politics and public discourse centres around the use of persuasion and influence in a responsible, sincere, and motivated manner, motivated by a genuine desire to enhance the wellbeing of the group. We can promote a more equitable and inclusive society that thrives on open communication and reasoned decisionmaking by respecting democratic norms, embracing openness, and appealing to common ambitions.

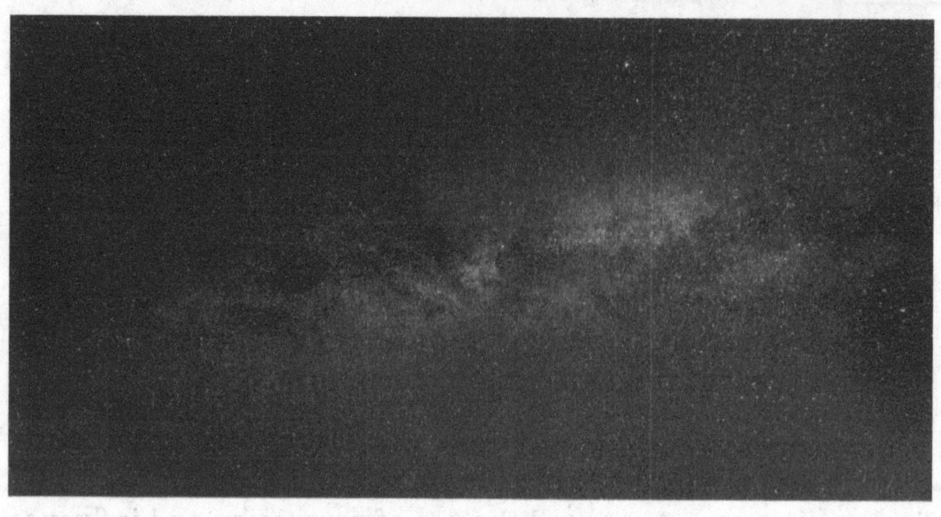

CONCLUSION:

1. Embracing The Ethical Machiavellian Mindset:

Ah, dear reader, the subtleties of doing so in personal relationships are like the dance of light on the sea profound and delicate. As you set out on this noble road, keep in mind that the art of influence must be used with the utmost care and compassion since the seeds of ethical manipulation can be sowed only within the confines of trust and honesty.

Take care of the empathy and understanding soil in the garden of relationships. Try to understand the thoughts and feelings of others nearby while enjoying each person's own personality. Your intentions can only be driven by the desire to inspire and empower others when you genuinely connect with them on a heartfelt level.

Dear reader, the foundation of this trip is patience. Avoid acting hastily while using your influence since doing so might result in unforeseen effects. Instead, spend time learning about the currents that run through each person's heart and let your impact be like the calm wind that gently sways a tree's leaves.

Honesty and transparency must be the guiding lights that show you the way. Do not let the gloom of lying obscure your intentions since trust is the tenuous cord that connects people's hearts. When you speak honestly, your words will carry the weight of authenticity, creating understanding and establishing ties that survive the test of time.

Be a source of inspiration and support in all your encounters. Encourage others to reach their own greatness by fanning their own inspiration's flames. Always keep in mind that helping people identify their own skills and abilities is more important than forcing them to conform to your will.

However, be careful not to fall victim to the tempting attraction of manipulation for personal benefit as you negotiate the landscape of ethical manipulation. Stay faithful to the principles that are at the center of who you are, and allow your moral compass serve as your compass for direction. This will help to ensure that your impact is firmly rooted in the pursuit of the greater good.

You could occasionally trip and fall on this path since human error is common. When you do, embrace humility, admitting your errors and making apologies while really repentant.

According to ancient sages, "To wield the power of influence ethically is to dance in harmony with the universe." May you lead the way for positive change and create a symphony of kindness and compassion in the lives of everyone you come in contact with.

Let grace, wisdom, and the brilliance of integrity guide you as you work to perfect the art of ethical manipulation in interpersonal interactions, dear reader.

2. Using Manipulation For Positive Change:

Ah, my reader, the pursuit of ethical influence bears significant relevance in the context of business and negotiations. Let's keep the knowledge of the past in mind as we negotiate the complex pathways of business and engagement, and let's aim for moral behavior.

It is crucial to consider how our actions could affect other people in these interactions. Build relationships based on respect and trust rather than manipulating or lying. Sustainable collaborations that last the test of time will be enabled by open and honest communication.

Dear reader, beware of the seduction of shady methods and quick cuts. Even while they can appear to offer quick advantages, they frequently result in longterm regret and a damaged image. Accepting the route of integrity can help you find your way through even the most difficult situations.

Keep in mind that negotiations are chances to seek mutual gain and peace rather than fights to be won at any costs. Look for areas of agreement, comprehension, and sympathetic care for the interests of all parties.

Develop empathy and compassion if you want to influence people in an ethical way. Recognize and respect other people's viewpoints and interests. By doing this, you may develop solutions that meet everyone's needs, encouraging cooperation and a sense of success.

Dear reader, embrace your inner strength, but utilize it wisely and righteously. Instead of controlling people, give them the tools they need to succeed. You will find your own rise to greater heights through elevating others.

The ability to manipulate is not the ultimate test of a great master of this craft, dear reader; rather, it is the ability to motivate constructive change. If you choose the right course, your influence will extend well beyond any bargaining table.

3. Ethical Boundaries And Responsibility:

Ah, my reader, the idea of ethical manipulation may appear counterintuitive when it comes to social impact efforts. Let's instead explore the fundamental knowledge that underlies this idea.

One must be cautious and alert when pursuing great goals. If there is such a thing as ethical manipulation, it should be used to achieve beneficial results for the greater benefit. This calls for a strong sense of accountability and a sincere dedication to the well-being of the people we want to serve.

Let us keep in mind that manipulation is not necessarily bad as we begin these activities. Its moral standing is determined by the motivation behind its usage. As a result, dear reader, our motivations must be driven by empathy, compassion, and a sincere desire to improve both society as a whole and individual lives.

Any social impact program should continue to be guided by the notion of transparency. We must be open and honest about our goals, processes, and anticipated results. Gaining the confidence of our stakeholders guarantees that our decisions are made with honesty and that our actions are consistent with our stated objectives.

The ethical use of manipulation also means giving individuals we want to assist more power, dear reader. We should promote their agency and autonomy rather than forcing our will on them. Since the impacted communities take on a more active role in shaping their own development, this empowerment may result in longlasting transformation.

We must guard against the desire to manipulate for our own benefit or to promote secret objectives as we walk this fine line, though. Individual interests should never take precedence over the welfare of others. Keep in mind that improving society is the ultimate goal of all of our efforts.

Let us embrace humility and lifelong learning as we work to perfect the art of ethical manipulation for good, dear reader. Keep an open mind to other viewpoints since it is only through cooperation and group knowledge that we can actually bring about dramatic change.

In conclusion, remember that ethical manipulation may have a beneficial effect when used with good intentions, despite the fact that it may seem counterintuitive. Let us use this power carefully as we work to make the world a better and more just place for everyone, always conscious of the moral ramifications of our choices.

4. Mastering Ethical Manipulation For A Better

World:

Dear Reader, the idea of ethical manipulation in political and public conversation is one that is difficult and complex. Even while the word "manipulation" frequently conjures up negative images, there are times when it may be used morally to advance the interests of society and encourage constructive change.

Political manipulation that adheres to the ethics of truthfulness, openness, and respect for democratic norms involves the art of persuasion and influence. Instead than seeking to confuse or mislead the audience, it focuses on enabling people to make educated decisions.

The ethical use of speech and message is a key component of political manipulation. Leaders and public personalities must be careful with their words and arguments, making sure they are based in reality and not motivated by malice or selfish interests. Honest communication builds trust, and trust is the cornerstone of a successful democracy.

Additionally, ethical manipulation entails appealing to societal norms and ambitions that are held in common. Instead of fostering division or sowing dissension, leaders who want to see good change can encourage optimism, unity, and a feeling of purpose among their followers.

Maintaining moral standards in politics and public debate requires transparency. Gaining the public's trust requires leaders to be transparent about their intentions, objectives, and decision-making procedures. Disillusionment and societal division can result from hidden goals and covert tactics, which undermine democracy at its core.

A strong dedication to critical thinking and abstaining from manipulation for one's own advantage or immediate success are also necessary for ethical manipulation. Instead, it emphasizes long-term viable solutions that take into account the actual demands and concerns of the populace.

As citizens, it is our duty to hold our elected officials responsible for their words and deeds. To protect the credibility of our political institutions and public debate, we must be vigilant against deceptive strategies that undercut the democratic process.

Ultimately, dear reader, ethical manipulation in politics and public discourse centres around the use of persuasion and influence in a responsible, sincere, and motivated manner, motivated by a genuine desire to enhance the wellbeing of the group. We can promote a more equitable and inclusive society that thrives on open communication and reasoned decisionmaking by respecting democratic norms, embracing openness, and appealing to common ambitions.

EPILOGUE

As "Ethical Machiavellian: Mastering the Art of Manipulation for Good" comes to an end, it is crucial to take stock of our joint transformational journey. In search of a balance that advances society as a whole, we have investigated the complex dance between morality and manipulation across these pages. We have successfully handled the complexity of power relationships, persuasion, and influence while maintaining a firm commitment to moral standards.

We examined the wisdom of historical people and current philosophers in the chapters that came before, learning from both traditional Machiavellian tactics and cutting-edge ethical views. In personal interactions, professional pursuits, or larger social situations, we have seen how the art of manipulation may be used to effect beneficial change. Our research has been informed by the knowledge that, when used wisely and morally, manipulation may serve as a weapon for empowerment rather than oppression.

Keep in mind as we leave ways that being an ethical Machiavellian is not without its difficulties. It calls for a keen awareness of one's motivations, a thorough knowledge of human psychology, and a dedication to honesty and justice. The traditional binary of good and evil is transcended by ethical Machiavellianism, which challenges us to traverse the gray areas present in our decision-making.

Adopting the ethical Machiavellian principles entails appreciating the power of persuasion and using it to advance good causes, uplift people, and reform rigid structures. It involves using a steady hand to control the power currents and directing our strategic thinking down avenues that promote growth and prosperity for everybody.

Keep in mind that education is your best ally as you continue your path as an ethical Machiavellian. Continue strengthening your communication skills, human behavior comprehension, and capacity to influence situations while maintaining your integrity. People with wisdom, empathy, and a strong commitment to the welfare of others are needed to direct the course of events in the world.

Let this book's last chapter usher in a new chapter in your own life, one in which you embrace your responsibility as a force for good, a champion of justice, and a master of ethical manipulation. May your deeds create a legacy of empowerment, justice, and change that reverberates across society.

sincereest regards,

~Mohd Faisal

ABOUT THE AUTHOR

Mohd Faisal

Mohd Faisal as an Indian author has penned several motivational books such as "The Ikigai Blueprints", "39 Commandments for Financial Success", and "Dark Triad Unmasked" etc. His books have helped thousands of readers across the globe to take control of their lives and achieve their dreams. His books offer practical advice and  actionable strategies for overcoming obstacles and achieving success in all areas of life.

His unique perspective and engaging writing style have earned him a loyal following of readers who appreciate his practical approach to personal growth and financial management. His books are an invaluable resource for achieving your goals.

BOOKS BY THIS AUTHOR

39 Hidden Commandments: For Financial Success, Money Making And Stress-Free Life.

Are you tired of feeling stressed and unfulfilled in your life? Are you ready to take control of your finances and relationships? Look no further than "39 Hidden Commandments for Financial Success, Stress-Free Life, and Self-Actualization, Better Family and Social Relationships."

In this book, you'll discover practical, actionable advice to help you achieve your goals and live your best life. From creating a budget and building wealth to improving your communication skills and nurturing your relationships, these commandments will guide you every step of the way.

With witty and relatable anecdotes, this book will not only educate but also entertain and inspire you. You'll learn the importance of self-care, time management, and goal-setting, and how to apply these concepts to your own life.

So, whether you're a recent graduate just starting out or a seasoned professional looking to improve your life, "39 Hidden Commandments for Financial Success, Stress-Free Life" is the ultimate guide to achieving your dreams and living a fulfilling life.

Dark Triad - Unmasked: Understanding And Avoiding Narcissism, Machiavellianism, And

Psychopathy

Have you ever wondered what makes some people so charming and charismatic while others are just plain manipulative and toxic? Well, look no further because "The Dark Triad: Unmasked Understanding and Avoiding Narcissism, Machiavellianism, and Psychopathy" has got you covered!

In this book, we'll take a deep dive into the world of the Dark Triad - a group of personality traits that are commonly associated with narcissism, Machiavellianism, and psychopathy. But don't worry, we won't be throwing around big words and complicated theories. Instead, we'll be using a conversational style to help you understand these concepts in a fun and engaging way.

You'll learn all about the different traits that make up the Dark Triad, from grandiose narcissism to ruthless Machiavellianism to cold-hearted psychopathy. We'll explore how these traits manifest in different types of people, and how you can spot them in your own life.

But more than just identifying the Dark Triad in others, we'll also help you understand how these traits can show up in your own personality. That's right - you might just be a little bit Dark Triad yourself! But don't worry, we won't judge you. Instead, we'll give you practical tips and advice for managing these traits and becoming a better, more empathetic person.

So whether you're looking to avoid toxic relationships, improve your own personality, or just have a good laugh at the expense of some truly awful people, "The Dark Triad: Unmasked Understanding and Avoiding Narcissism, Machiavellianism, and Psychopathy" is the book for you. Let's dive in!

The Ikigai Blueprint For A Rich And Fulfilling Life.:

The Secrets To Financial Freedom.

"The Ikigai Blueprint: For A Rich And Fulfilling Life" is a guidebook that delves into the Japanese concept of Ikigai and provides a roadmap for finding purpose and fulfillment in life.

Based on the teachings of the Japanese island of Okinawa, the book explores the four key elements of Ikigai - what you love, what you are good at, what the world needs, and what you can be paid for - and shows how these elements can be combined to create a fulfilling life.

The book combines practical advice, inspiring stories, and thought-provoking exercises to help readers find their own personal Ikigai and live a life filled with joy, purpose, and meaning. Whether you are seeking to improve your career, deepen your relationships, or simply live a more fulfilling life, "The Ikigai Blueprint" provides a blueprint for creating a life of abundance, happiness, and purpose.

~ THE END ~

~ THE END ~